WORLD TREASURE

BAMBERG

A Guide to the Historic Old City with day trips in the region

This panel painting (ca. 1483) by Ludwig Katzheimer the Elder depicts the "Apostles' Farewell". The view of Bamberg in the background is considered to be one of the earliest depictions of a medieval city.

Text:	Wolfgang Kootz
Photographs:	Willi Sauer, Ingeborg Limmer, Reinhold Lippert

Kraichgau Verlag

Welcome to Bamberg

The first thing a city needs to surpass other cities in beauty is an attractive location. In this department, Bamberg has several advantages over its many rivals. It blends harmoniously into a landscape with seven hills – like ancient Rome – above the wide Regnitz River Valley shortly before the river flows into the Main. On account of this location, the numerous religious communities, and the town's early importance as the seat of a prince-bishop, Bamberg was once known as "the Rome of Germany". Moreover, Bamberg had the good fortune to survive, always more or less unscathed, the numerous wars fought during its long history, as a result of which the old town is largely intact. Today, for this reason, the city is considered a European architectural historical monument. In 1993, this impressive area measuring 250 ha was placed under the protection of UNESCO as an international cultural treasure. This makes Bamberg one of 12 sites in Germany and 400 worldwide that have been recognised in this manner.

View from the tower of Geyerswörth Palace with the most striking buildings of the Old Town: in the foreground the Town Hall; to the

Outstanding buildings include the Late Romantic Imperial Cathedral with the world-famous "Bamberg Rider", the Baroque New Residence with its Rose Garden and an incomparable view of the Michaelsberg ("St. Michael's Mountain"), the completely pre-served Old Household, the Old Bridge Town Hall in the middle of the left fork of the Regnitz River, and the picturesque row of old fis-hermen's houses on the riverbank, known as "Little Venice". Thus historic medieval architecture has survived here in abundance, enri-ched by numerous magnificent structures of the Baroque era, when Balthasar Neumann and the Dientzenhofer brothers served as master builders under the Prince-Bishops of Schönborn. Bamberg emerged from a settlement around the fortress of the Babenberger Dynasty, which gave the city its name. When this dynasty died out, the settlement and fortress rever-ted to the crown. Emperor Heinrich II. wanted to make it his capital, founded the bishopric, endowed numerous institutions, and led the community to initial prosperity. Numerous churches and religious communities arose

left, the Cathedral and the New Residence; to the right, in the back-ground, the Monastery of St. Michael

during this time. Bamberg remained the residence of an independent principality until 1802.

Even today, the city is the seat of an archbishop and the centre of a diocese as successor to the former bishopric. It has 70,000 inhabitants and ranks first among the industrial centres of Upper Franconia, but its main attraction is still as a centre of occidental culture. Incredible treasures are kept behind the walls of its historic buildings: besides the aforementioned rider, these include the grave of Emperor Heinrich and Empress Kunigunde, the only remaining papal grave north of the Alps, St. Otto's Tomb, the gold-embroidered cloak, papal vestments, and "Günthertuch" of the 11th century. The textiles mentioned, as well as other Cathedral treasures, can be seen in the Diocesan Museum. Among the many other museums, the Old Household and the New Residence in particular hold unexpected treasures. It is no surprise to find this rich historical legacy reflected in the world of business: the city landscape is enlivened by more than 20 antiquities dealers and art shops as well as 10 galleries. In terms of cultural offerings, the Bamberg Symphony has established itself as a leading symphony since 1946, when it was founded by displaced musicians from the German Philharmonic in Prague as well as musicians from Carlsbad and Silesia. Besides this, the E.T.A.-Hoffmann Theatre, the Brentano Theatre, and Lohse's Marionette Theatre, the Bamberger Cabaret Days, and the Calderón open-air productions are theatrical highlights.

Bamberg is by no means an open-air museum with overage inhabitants, as evidenced by the numerous pupils and the 8500 students at Bamberg University (founded in 1972) seen throughout the city each day. They liven up the streets and squares, especially the pedestrian zone, which is not just for shoppers. It stretches from the Bridge Town Hall to the Green Market. From here it is just a few metres to Maxplatz, where fresh fruit and vegetables are offered daily, with regional specialities on Saturdays.

Of course the numerous restaurants also offer specialities: grilled sausage and "Blue Tips", Bamberg onions and Franconian Sauerbraten, accompanied above all by local beer from one of the city's nine remaining breweries (there were still 65 in 1818!). The most notable of the more than 50 types offered is the famous Rauchbier ("smoky beer") that is served in practically every restaurant and pub in Bamberg. With a brewing tradition this rich, it is understandably difficult for the otherwise so popular Franconian wine to gain a foothold here.

Above all else, tourists who come to Bamberg should come prepared to take their time exploring the city, given the rich variety of things to see and do here. Besides a campground and 20 caravan lots, there are nearly 2000 beds available in hotels and inns of all categories. Underground garages and car parks offer shelter for cars, making exploring the city by foot or with public transportation a more attractive option for drivers. There are special offers for tourists, for example, the tourist tikket good for 48 hours on all routcs or the somewhat more expensive Bamberg Card, which additionally includes a guided tour of the city, admission to some museums, and a daily newspaper. Besides this, the Bamberg Tourist Information Office offers guided tours of the Old Town daily, as well as tours of the Domberg, the Residence, the Cathedral, and the Diocesan Museum, day trips to Vierzehnheiligen and Banz Monastery as well as Ebrach Monastery and Weißenstein Palace, many suggestions and maps for hikers, bicyclists, and motorists, as well as schedules listing special events such as public festivals, markets, open-air theatres, concerts, theatre performances, antique weeks, the Christmas Market, and the crèche displays at Easter and Christmas.

How to Use this Book

We have divided up the sights of Bamberg's Old Town into two tours, both of which start and end near the centrally located Old Bridge Town Hall. The first tour, the longer of the two, takes the reader up through the southern part of the isle city to the Bergstadt neighbourhood of the bishops with its numerous churches, monasteries, and convents, middle-class homes and cannons' courts, the Cathedral, the Old Household, and the New Residence, then back down to the banks of the Regnitz and a unique view of "Little Venice". In short: this tour unites the highlights of the former capital city. Persons who are in a hurry and want to complete this route in a single morning or afternoon are advised not to spend too much time at the individual stops along the way.

The second tour takes us through the middle-class Isle Town with its numerous markets and the university district to the pedestrian precinct between the Green Market and the Bridge Town Hall, where one can round out one's visit to Bamberg with window shopping or in one of the numerous cosy restaurants.

A Bamberg Chronology

7th Century	There is a large fortress complex on the Domberg ("Cathedral Mountain")
902	The "castrum babenberg" is the possession of the East Franconian Babenberger Dynasty. When this dynasty dies out, the fief reverts to the Crown.
973	Emperor Otto II gives the fortress and settlement "papinberc" to Heinrich the Quarrelsome, Duke of Bavaria, as a present.
995	The later King Heinrich II inherits the Bamberg Estate upon the demise of his father Heinrich the Quarrelsome.
997	Heinrich II and his wife Kunigunde stay in Bamberg.
1002	Heinrich II is crowned King.
1007	Heinrich II founds the Bishopric of Bamberg. He intends to make the town the capital of his kingdom. Numerous churches and religious communities spring up. Bamberg is capital of a principality until 1802.
1012	The "Imperial Cathedral" is consecrated.
1014	Heinrich II is crowned Emperor in Rome.
1024	Emperor Heinrich II dies.

A painting showing the founder of the Bishopric, Emperor Heinrich II

1046	Bishop Suitger (1040-47) becomes Pope (Clemens II) at the behest of Emperor Heinrich III. He dies after nine months, probably of unnatural causes.
1102-1139	Bishop Otto I. (canonised 1189) is called the "Apostle to the Pomeranians". He founds religious communities, has churches built, and acts as mediator during formulation of the Concordat of Worms.
1146	Heinrich II canonised.
1152	King Konrad III dies in Bamberg whilst returning from a crusade.
1185	The Imperial Cathedral is ravished by fire.
1200	Empress Kunigunde canonised.
1208	King Philipp of Swabia is beaten to death during a wedding party at the Household in Bamberg and is at first buried in the Cathedral (later reburied in the Imperial Cathedral in Speyer).
1215	The third Cathedral is built.
1237	The Late Romantic/Early Gothic cathedral is consecrated.
1430	Hussite invasion. The defenceless Town of Bamberg must pay a high ransom for its safety.
15th Century	The Cloister Precincts (Immunities) have their own jurisprudence and thus do not pay municipal taxes. This is repeatedly a bone of contention with the city. Consequentially, many wealthy patrician families move away, followed by the artists.
1525	Peasants' Revolt: Bamberg citizens plunder the Courts of the Cannons and St. Michael's Monastery. The revolt is put down with the help of the Swabian Federation, the ringleaders are hung.
1553	Margrave Albrecht Alcibiades of Brandenburg/Kulmbach conquers Bamberg. He extorts payments for protection, has the Courts of the Cathedral Cannons plundered, and permits his followers to lay waste to the Old Fortress.
1623-33	Witch burnings reach their zenith under Bishop Johann Georg II. Fuchs of Dornheim. Alone in the Bamberg District, the hysteria costs 600 people their lives.
1618-48	Thirty Year's War: The weakly fortified city is occupied and plundered and its inhabitants tormented repeatedly by troops from various sides. Due to the war and epidemics, Bamberg former

Prince-Bishop
Lothar Franz
von Schönborn
(1655-1729).

	population of 12,000 is reduced by nearly half.
1693-1746	Prince-Bishops Lothar Franz and Friedrich Karl von Schönborn promote commerce, skilled trades, and manufacturing. This is Bamberg's Golden Era. The Baroque capital takes shape in the form by which it is known today.
1802	The Principality/Bishopric of Bamberg is dissolved and devolves to Bavaria.
1808	E.T.A. Hoffmann becomes Director of Music.
1817	Bamberg becomes an Archbishopric.
1841	The Ludwig-Donau-Main Canal is opened.
1844	The railway reaches Bamberg.
1914-18	First World War: 1330 Bamberg natives are killed in action.
1933-45	Third Reich and Second World War: The approx. 1000 Jewish citizens of the city are expelled or murdered, 3700 Bamberg natives are killed or missing in action, another 378 people perish as a result of air attacks during the final year of the war.
1981	Bamberg is declared to be an urban monument.
1993	The city, which now boasts some 70,000 inhabitants, is added to UNESCO's List of "World Treasures of Humanity".

A Tour of the Historic Old Town

Geyerswörth Palace ①

The underground parking garage "Geyerswörth" is ideal for those tourists who arrive in the Old Town by car, especially since the Tourist Information Office is just a few steps away. The Tourist Information Office, together with the City Office of Social Services, is located in one-time Geyerswörth Palace (1). This was the dynastic fortress of the patrician Geyer family, which also held the river island (= Wörth). In 1580, the Bishopric of Bamberg acquired the grounds and buildings. The obsolete buildings were razed and replaced by a five-winged construction (1585-87) according to plans by Master Builder Erasmus Braun. Thereafter the palace served as the residence of Prince-Bishops and a symbol of their status before being relegated to obscurity by the New Residence completed in 1705.

A pedestrian bridge in front of Geyerswörth Palace

Geyerswörth Palace:
The key to the tower can be borrowed from the Tourist Information Office Mon.-Thurs. 9:00 AM – 4:00 PM and Fri. 9:00 AM – 12:30 PM.

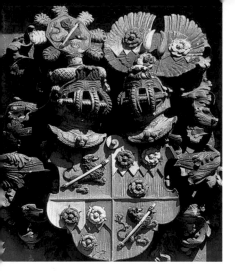

The coat-of-arms of the Prince-Bishop above the entrance to Geyerswörth Palace

The portal to the inner courtyard is adorned by the coat-of-arms of Prince-Bishop Ernst von Mengersdorf (1583-91), during whose regency the palace was constructed. The original city coat-of-arms from the neighbouring Old Town Hall is tucked away under the arcades of the atmospheric inner courtyard. Regrettably, nothing remains of the once magnificent furnishings; only parts of the Renaissance hall of 1605 were reconstructed. Today the city uses this room, which is decorated with figurative representations of the arts and sciences, for formal receptions; unfortunately, it is not open to the public. A climb to the top of the Palace Tower (137 stairs!), on the other hand, is well worth the effort. Its heights afford a magnificent view of the Old Town, with the Upper and Lower Bridges and the Old Town Hall in the foreground, the Domberg, the New Residence, and the four-towered cathedral behind them, and St. Michael's Mountain and the former Benedictine Monastery of St. Michael on the horizon. Interested tourists can borrow the key to the tower at the Tourist Information Office.

Old Town Hall ②

Opposite the courtyard portal, the Geyerwörthsteg crosses the Regnitz. From here, one has a unique view of the Old Town Hall (2). In Bamberg, it is also known as the island or bridge town hall, since it was built on an artificial island in the river and is connected to the banks by two bridges each. A Town Hall on this particular site was mentioned already in 1386; the present edifice was constructed starting in 1461 after city fire (1460). The half-timbered addition to the south side of the building (1668), the "Rottmeisterhäuschen", retains its original form to this day. Legend explains the unusual construction site with the Bishop's refusal to grant the citizens a building site for the Town Hall that they demanded. It

The Old Town Hall, also known as "Island Town Hall", between the spans of the bridges over the Regnitz. At the front is the "Rottmeisterhäuschen" (1668).

seems more likely, however, that the self-confident citizens wanted to demonstrate their newfound power on the border between their isle city and the Bishop's city on the hill. A glance upstream from the bridge reveals the one-time Mill District (flour, paper, and bark mills, today hotels and a students' dormitory). A crucifixion group (1715) stands on the Upper

The stairway to the Upper Bridge, which leads through the Baroque gatetower of the Old Town Hall to the Isle Town.

Bridge. Through the right arch of this bridge, it is possible to see the bank of the Regnitz with its romantic fishermen's houses, known locally as "Little Venice".

At the end of the footbridge, we keep to the right and reach the Western end of the Upper Bridge. The imposing Town Hall Spire rises before us; it was built by order of Prince-Bishop Friedrich Karl von Schönborn (1729-46) under the direction of the famous master builder Balthasar Neumann. It was encased in Baroque style and adorned with a cupola. The very ornate balconies and coats-of-arms were added by sculptor Joseph Bonaventura Mutschele after 1750. The municipal coat-of-arms facing the Cathedral shows St. George as a knight, the adjacent facade is an impressive painted illusion in Baroque style that refers to the 1753 death of Prince-Bishop Philipp Anton von Frankenstein. His successor Konrad von Stadion had the Baroque conversion completed and had his own coat-of-arms affixed to the balcony on the Isle Town side. His arrival in Bamberg is also the subject of the frescoes on the neighbouring wall. The spatial effect of the work created by Johann Anwander starting in 1755 is achieved above all through the addition of shadows

The Ludwig Collection at Old Town Hall:
Tue. – Sun. 9:30 AM – 4:30 PM
Tel.: 0951/87 18 71; Fax: 87 14 64

Old Town Hall, Ludwig Collection:
A 18th century porcelain plate from Meißen.

and plastic elements. Thus careful observers will notice, as a symbol of painting, an angel whose leg extends out of the wall. Elsewhere, this type of design is used only in indoor spaces.

Since 1995, the rooms of the former Town Hall have housed the collection of the chocolate manufacturer Ludwig in an exhibit entitled "The Splendour of the Baroque". This is one of the most extensive private collections of porcelain in Europe and simultaneously one of the largest collections of Strasbourg faiences. While exploring the museum, visitors also have an opportunity to view the spacious staircase and the former town council chambers. Known today as the "Rococo Hall", the city administration now uses it, like the Renaissance Hall in Geyerswörth Palace, for receptions.

The Upper Bridge, which leads through the Town Hall Tower, was created in this form in 1453, but had to be replaced frequently. From here there is a lovely view of, among other sights, Geyerswörth Palace as well as St. Stephen's Church (recognisable by its onion spire) and the Church of Our Lady, known as the "Upper Parish Church ". Upstream on the right bank of the Regnitz stand two old iron cranes and behind these the gabled facade of the Old Slaughterhouse (1741/42), which is decorated with a sculpture of an oxen. Together with an attached new annex, today it is used as a university library.

The fishermen's houses of Bamberg's "Little Venice" form rows just behind this building. The crucifixion group over the middle pier was created in 1715 by sculptor J. L. Gollwitzer. Regrettably, the Lower Bridge just a few meters away was replaced by a plain, austere bridge after the original was destroyed in 1945. One of five figures is all that remains of its predecessors: St. Kunigunde, the wife of Heinrich II. However, this is the Bamberg residsents' favourite statue.

Am Schillerplatz ③

From the Upper Bridge, we return to Geyerswörth by the previous way. Here we keep to the left and follow a footpath along the water with a view of romantic half-timbered buildings. Finally, we leave the island via the arched wooden bridge, from which we follow the route Habergasse (to the right)/Generalsgasse/Zinkenwörth. The last-mentioned leads us after just a few steps to Schillerplatz (3). On the east side of this square is the City Theatre (erected 1808) at

painter and master machinist, piano and singing instructor, and also stage director and theatrical composer. On the side, he was also employed as a music journalist and later as a writer who helped to earn international recognition for German Romanticism. Ideals and reality often mingle in his works. During his Bamberg Period (1808-1813), he immortalised among others the talking dog" Berganza" in the Hain – the manicured park on the Regnitz -, the Capuchin Monastery, the doorknob "Little Apple Woman", his garret apartment "Poet's Room" as

Schillerplatz with monument and City Theatre.

which Bamberg's most famous allround artist, E.T.A. Hoffmann, first worked as musical director for a brief time. After being forced to resign, held the posts of scenery

well as, idealised, his passionate, unfilled love for his singing pupil Julia Marc, which nearly drove him mad. E.T.A. Hoffmann lived at Schillerplatz opposite the theatre in a narrow house that today houses a rather modest museum in his honour.

The Richard-Wagner-Straße marks the southeast boundary of Schillerplatz. A quick side trip to the left over to Hainstraße and there again a few meters to the left leads to Villa Dessauer (No. 4a), built in 1883 as one of the most splendid houses of the 19th century. It has been restored and today houses the Municipal Gallery, which makes modern art – especially by local artists – accessible to the public.

Villa Dessauer, built in Neo-Renaissance style in 1884, today houses the Municipal Gallery of Modern Art.

E.T.A. Hoffmann House: May – Oct.: *Tues. – Fri. 4:00-6:00 PM, Sat., Sun., and holidays 10:00 AM – Noon.*
Municipal Gallery Villa Dessauer: *Open year round for special exhibitions. Tel. 0951/871861 Fax: 871464*

Concordia Palace ④

From Schillerplatz, Richard-Wagner-Straße and the Nonnenbrücke ("Nuns' Bridge") lead us along the old canal to the banks of the Regnitz, which we follow for a short distance to the left. Picturesquely situated on the opposite bank is the Baroque moated castle "Concordia" (4), which Counsellor Ignaz Tobias Böttinger had built by Master Builder Johann Dientzenhofer during the period 1716-22. Dientzenhofer directed construction of the palace of the Prince-Bishops in Pommersfelden at the same time; a certain stylistic similarity between the two

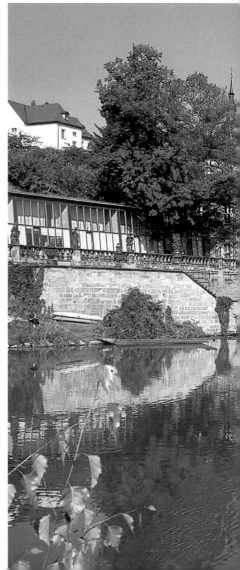

A view across the Regnitz to "Concordia" Palace, built 1716-22 for Councillor Böttinger.

works does not escape the eye. The elegant two-winged palace and its garden face the river, to which they are connected by a flight of steps. In this way, it was easy for host and guests to go punting on the river during the garden parties that were typical at the time.

A little further upstream, the Mühlwörth leads to the Oberen Mühlbrücke ("Upper Mill Bridge"), via which we leave the island. Following Concordiastraße to the left will bring us to the city palace of the same name, which was just described above. Today it houses the International Artists' House Villa Concordia. Here approximately one dozen scholarship holders in the fields of music, fine arts, and literature work and present their readings, concerts, and exhibitions to the public.

Böttingerhaus ⑤

Now we walk down Concordia-straße in the opposite direction until we reach its starting point, where the Untere Stefansberg branches off steeply to the left. Here is the abundantly ornamented Böttingerhaus (5), the high official's first palace, built 1707-13. At the end of his life and carrier, he was entitled to use the following: "Licentiate of Law, Royal Bambergian Privy Councillor, Directorial Envoy to the Franconian Circle, Spiritual Advisor, Vice-President of the Tax Collection Office, Director of the Imperial Regional Court" and "Barracks Director". Besides drawing what was probably a considerable salary, he also profited from having grown up in an affluent family, his wife's handsome dowry, and the gifts of money that were customarily made to high officials at the time. Thus he already bought the lot in the Judenstraße back in 1701, the same year in which he took a wife. The Prince-Bishop generously promoted the construction project by providing the construction materials free of charge, as he did with all buildings that served to beautify his capital city. An anecdote illustrates just how far the official support for this project went. When the nobles of the neighbouring von Staufenberg family brought suit in vain because of the gabled windows and a row of trees near the boundary of the property, Böttinger instead erected a wall that obscured the neighbours' windows out even more effectively. It still stands today.

Despite massive investment and employment of the Prince-Bishop's master builder, the building decidedly does not reflect the fashion of the times. It lacks spacious grounds and thus separation from the neighbours, as well as the spacious garden and the fashionably clear organisation in the style of the French Baroque, according to which the Prince-Bishop had his buildings constructed. This was compounded by damp walls because the palace was situated on a slope, a cold apartment due to the open, Italian-style staircase, and a shortage of space due the rapidly rising number of family members – for after all, the Böttingers had twelve children. All this caused him to have the already mentioned new mansion built on the Regnitz, just two short years after completion of the palace, which was decorated inside with costly leather wall coverings, inlaid floors, stucco work and murals.

▲ *The Böttingerhaus, Councillor Böttinger's first palace, built 1707-13 in the style of an Italian Palazzo.*

◀ *Böttingerhaus: A Baroque doorknocker.*

19

*The picturesque
inner courtyard of
the Böttingerhaus.*

The Church of St. Stephan ⑥

After taking just a few steps up the
Stephansberg ("St. Stephan's
Mountain"), we turn to the right
and climb the steps to the Church
of St. Stephan (6). The original
church on this site was founded by
Emperor Heinrich II and his wife
Kunigunde, who wanted to turn
Bamberg into a second Rome.
There, besides the world-famous
St. Peter's Basilica, there is also a
church known as Santo Stefano
Rotondo (5th century). Thus in
Bamberg, too, the Cathedral was

dedicated to St. Peter and shortly
thereafter the Church of St.
Stephan was consecrated. Like its
Roman namesake, it is a centrali-
sed building in the form of a Greek
cross. Empress Kunigunde donated the land for the church, the
cathedral chapter, and other tracts
of land from her "Morgengabe",
the lands that she received as a
wedding present. It was the only
church north of the Alps to be consecrated by a Pope, namely by
Pope Benedict VIII who stayed

with Emperor Heinrich in Bamberg for a political summit in 1020.

All that remains of the original building is the foundation walls and thus the ground plan. The tower, which today is the oldest architectural element, still evidences Romanesque forms in its lower storeys, above these two early Gothic storeys (13th century), and finally the elegant Baroque top. Work on the Baroque edifice still in existence today began during the Thirty Years' War, but the available funds were soon exhausted due to the nature of those hard times. Thus it took from 1626 until 1680 to refurbish the choir and the three naves. The planned cupola in the crossing was ultimately dispensed with entirely, being replaced instead by a flat ceiling with a relief portraying the martyrdom of St. Stephan.

Until 1803, the Church of St. Stephan was the centre of a separate governmental district subject only to the Emperor, an "Immunity District" with its own legislation and tax laws, the "ruler" of which was the Provost. Secularisation, the political reorganisation under Napoleon, also stripped the religious community and Church of St. Stephan of their functions. Until 1808, the church was plundered for its rich furnishings and misused as a warehouse before being turned over for use by the Protestant congregation. The main sights of interest inside are above all the richly populated Baroque organ front (1695) and the

Church of St. Stephen: High altar and choir stalls (1769).

Baroque organ front (1695).

A relief of the church's founder, Empress Kunigunde.

to the church, where Empress Kunigunde is again depicted as founder of the Church of St. Stephan. This is where she lived whenever staying in Bamberg without the Emperor.

Behind the sanctuary, opposite the steps described earlier, we come to the narrow street "Eisgrube", which we follow to the right. House No. 14, mentioned already in 1299, is home to Bamberg's most famous doorknob, the "Little Apple Woman". Romantic author E.T.A. Hoffmann immortalised it in his work "The Golden Pot".

Rococo-style choir stalls (1769). The columns behind the high altar (the stoning of St. Stephan) depict Empress Kunigunde as founder of the church and her husband, Emperor Heinrich II, as founder of the cathedral. Unlike the cathedral canons, the canons of the religious community did not have to be of noble descent. They for the most part had their houses in the nearby church district. This is also where the women's religious community stood opposite the main entrance

In the "Eisgrube": The "Little Apple Woman" doorknob.

Parish "Church of Our Lady" ⑦

The Eisgrube ends in front of the parish "Church of Our Lady" (7), known in Bamberg as the "Upper Parish Church". The two-story apartment with a plain cupola (1535) atop the tower stands in stark contrast to the harmonious tracery of the tower.

The Upper Parish Church is on the territory of the settlement known as "papinberc" that Emperor Otto II assigned together with the fortress to Heinrich the Quarrelsome, Duke of Bavaria in 973. There was a chapel here in the 9th century, which was replaced a little less than 200 years later by a Romanesque church. Construction of the present church began around 1300 and was finally completed in 1535. Changes were made during the Baroque period, affecting, above all, the shape of the windows and the roof of the choir.

Other items of interest on the north side, which we follow to the left, include a wooden crucifix (ca. 1500), a Baroque Johannes Nepomuk, a Gothic Madonna (14th century, both carved in stone) as well as few older gravestones (from 1500 on). They show that the parish burying grounds

The parish "Church of Our Lady", usually called "Upper Parish Church". In front of the aisle is a roofed Mount of Olives scene.

Artistic monuments of interest line the outer facade. One special gem is the Bridal Door on the north side of the nave. In the multiple recesses under canopies, we recognise the 5 wise and 5 foolish virgins; the central field under the arch depicts the crowning of Mary. Two stone statues, Sts. Peter and Paul, flank the door.

extended around the church here until well into the 19th century. At the tower are two stunningly executed stone sculptures portraying the St. John the Evangelist and the Visitation of Mary. Walking past additional gravestones on the south side of the church, we come to the main entrance on the west side. Next to the door is another

Upper Parish Church: A view down the Baroque nave to the choir and the high altar, which surrounds a miraculous image.

Gothic Madonna (ca. 1360) as well as, off to the side slightly, two scenes from the Mount of Olives, one with a roof, and the other a so-called Angsttafel or "panel of dread".

Countless works make the church interior a treasure-chest of sacred art and bear witness to the popular piety of past centuries. Figures of the apostles (15th century), together with Christ, decorate the columns in the nave and guide the eye toward the high altar. It was created in 1714 as a donation from Prince-Bishop Lothar Franz von Schönborn and holds a miracle-working image that is still revered today, an enthroned Madonna (ca. 1320). Thus this altar, surrounded by numerous side altars and ancillary altars, stands not only at the centre of the church but also at the centre of the city's reverence for Mary. Every year on the Sunday after Ascension Day, the festively arrayed Madonna is borne in a formal procession to the pained Mother of God in St.-Martin's Church.

One feature typical of pilgrimage churches is the choir gallery, which was especially important for channelling streams of pilgrims' days of remembrance. Here alone there are six ancillary altars, which like the others were used as pilgrimage and intercessory altars for the cares of day-to-day life. The Sacristy (1392) at the head of the choir holds a wealth of individual depictions, including figures of the disciples and evangelists on three storeys. The most impressive decorations, however, are those of the middle axis with (from bottom to top) the Burial of Christ, the latticed sacramental niche, the Face of Christ and the Last Judgement: in the imagery of the Middle Ages, this was an urgent appeal to the faithful to conduct their lives according to the teachings of Christ. One of the most original works of art is located in a niche next to the Sacristy, a Gothic depiction of St. Anne in confinement after giving birth. The baptismal font (ca. 1520) is also artistically important and rich in meaning. The wooden panelling of the font depicts the Baptism of Christ and the seven sacraments.

On the way back to the main sanctuary, we pass the two lovely altars at the choir transept, which were created at the same time as the high altar. From here we can look over to the elegantly curved Baroque pulpit and along the south row of columns. Behind them, in aisle, are additional important works of interest: the late Gothic groups of carvings with representation of the

Painting (1547/48) "Maria's Accession" by Jacopo Tintoretto.

Ascension and the Crowning of Mary as well as a painting (1547/48) by Jac. Tintoretto that also takes as its theme the Ascension of Mary. Regrettably, there simply isn't space here to mention many additional treasures such as statues, paintings, votive images, and epitaphs that wait to be discovered and interpreted by interested visitors.

The street "Unterer Kaulberg", to which we now descend, runs below the north side of the church. The Kaulberg was once the preferred living area of the winegrowers, who are called "hoers" in Franconia. The fashionable facade of house No. 4, flanked by gatehouses, belongs to the former New Ebracher Court (1765), a townhouse of the nearby Cistercian

Upper Parish Church: Wooden relief on the base of the baptismal font (ca. 1520).

Monastery at Ebrach. To the north it adjoins the enormous Old Ebracher Court (1682), where a St. Bernhard's Cross commemorates the founder of the order, Bernhard of Clairvaux.

The enormous gabled facade of the Old Erbracher Court (1682).

The Carmelite Monastery ⑧

Walking up the Unterer Kaulberg, after about 100 m we reach a small square with the Carmelite Monastery (8) and its church. In the 13th century, the Carmelites founded a monastery in Bamberg's Old Town, i.e., on the island. It, however, was until it was dissolved in 1554. The Carmelites used it from 1589 until secularisation in 1803; they were able to reacquire it in 1902 and retain possession of it to this day. During the period 1692 - 1707 the Carmelites had their church, which

The Carmelite Monastery: View from the Romanesque cloister toward the spire of the monastery church.

housed in a building that the Bishop needed for a newly created seminary (1586). As a replacement, the monks received the Monastery of St. Theodore, which was empty at the time and had served as a Cistercian monastery since the 12th century at its heart was a medieval edifice, converted in the Baroque style according to plans by Master Builder Johann Leonhard Dientzenhofer. The new ornamental facade with the main door was moved toward the town and the

Carmelite Monastery:
Open to visitors daily 8:30 – 11:30 AM and 2:30 – 5:30 PM

The cloister of the Carmelite Monastery

vacant square. It is one of the most important Baroque works of art in Bamberg. The statues to the left and right of the Madonna depict Sts. Joseph and Theodore; those in the upper storey show Sts. Albert of Sicily and Johannes Nepomuk. The free-standing figure on the gable is the Prophet Elijah, the ancestral father of the Carmelites.

After the 1803 Secularisation, all of the furnishings, including the numerous altars, were sold. Of the original valuable furnishings, the only ones which the Carmelites where able to repurchase after 1902 were an ancillary altar (alter of St.

Cloister: Mysterious Romanesque capitals give flight to viewers' fancies.

Joseph) and the pulpit (both ca. 1714). All other present-day furnishings are 20th century reproductions. The Cloister, however, which we reach via the monastery door, at the left in front of the ornamental facade, is well worth a visit. The Romanesque arches and columns that today account for the architectural charm of the imposing structure were not added to the cloister until the second half of the 14th century. Besides this, one is impressed by the immense variety of plastic capital ornaments and their often seemingly fantastic graphical content. The vaulting was added in the 15th century (east wing) and the Baroque period, which necessitated installation of sturdier pillars, without however destroying the harmony of the overall work.

Returning to the church, we walk along its north side. The remnants of the Romanesque structure are clearly discernible along the lower part of the masonry work at the window openings. This becomes even more pronounced along the West Facade. The bricked-up Romanesque "Lion Door" here is regrettably one of the most striking relics of this early epoch of construction.

The Imperial Cathedral ⑨

From the north side of the cloister quarter, a footpath leads down to the cathedral grounds. We follow this path to the right at first, until turning half-left to ascend to the Cathedral District by way of the streets Hinteren Bach and Vorderen Bach. Here we first encounter the broad-based Baroque Cathedral Chapter House, built 1730 under architect Balthasar Neumann. Its rooms and the Cathedral Cloister are home to the Diocesan Museum.

By the time that King Heinrich II received permission from the Electors of his kingdom to establish the Bishopric of Bamberg in 1007, an enormous church was already under construction. It was consecrated to St. Peter already in 1012, like its Roman model. Two fires (1081 and 1185), however, almost completely destroyed the structure of the Ottonian Period, so that only a few fragments of it are still preserved today. The present-day church arose during the first half of the 13th century as a compromise between the original Romanesque and the then current early Gothic style. The 18th century saw a change in the silhouette when one of the ridge turrets was removed and four towers were finished with uniform pointed spires.

Today the main facade of the Cathedral faces eastward toward the city centre. To the left of the Georgenchor ("Choir of St. George"), broad steps lead up the

The Imperial Cathedral: Four enormous spires make it easy to distinguish from the town's numerous other churches.

Adam's Door, which does not look very inviting with its jagged friezes. Indeed, in the early Middle Ages it was used as an exit for penitents who, like Adam from paradise, were ejected from the church. The statues that were once placed here are now housed in the neighbouring Diocesan Museum.

The counterpart is the Gate of Grace, which leads to the ground floor of the Northeast Tower and today is the main entrance to the church. The eightfold recess ends in a round Romanesque arch. The tympanum shows the enthroned Mother of God, flanked by the sainted Emperor and Empress Kunigunde, at right, the founders of the Cathedral, and the patron saints of the church, Sts. Peter and George. A Priest and a Bishop remain modestly on the fringes, whilst the donor of the gate, a crusader, kneels in prayer before the Madonna. Vestiges of colour remind the viewer of the former splendour of the artwork.

In front of the portal is a highly weathered stark animal sculpture, a "Cathedral toad". The result of the effects of weathering on the lions that once guarded the entrances, a legend has nevertheless sprung up concerning the

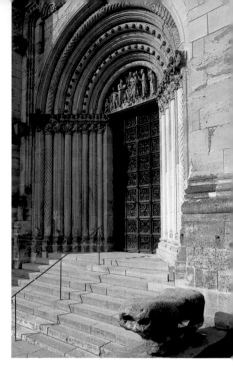

Today the Door of Grace is the main entrance to the Cathedral. In the left foreground is a "Cathedral Toad".

Cathedral toads. According to legend, the ambitious master of the West Choir pledged his soul to the devil if the devil would ensure that he was finished with his part of the cathedral before his colleague on the opposite side. At this, the devil put two toads in the foundation of the East Choir in order to delay construction. To commemorate this attack, so the legend goes,

Cathedral: Mon.-Fri.: April – Oct., 9:30 AM – 6:00 PM; Nov. – March, 9:30 AM – 5:00 PM.
Sat.: May – Oct., 9:30 – 11:45 AM and 12:35 – 5:00.
The cathedral is closed to tourists during religious services as well as from Maundy Thursday until the Saturday before Easter, on 29 June, 30 June, 1 Nov., 2 Nov., and Christmas Eve.

◀ *The head of the famous Bamberg Rider, whose identity, as well as that of his creator, is still a mystery to scholars.*

Imperial Cathedral: The ▶ Bamberg Rider, sculpted in the early 13th century by an anonymous master, embodied the ideal of a medieval ruler.

the stone toad figures were placed in front of the East Choir.

After passing through the Northeast Tower, we come to the stone choir stalls in the North Aisle. Three reliefs show the Annunciation, then the prophets are shown in groups of two. The gravestone of Pope Clemens II (died 1047) is attached to the first pillar to the left. As a Suitger, he was also the second Bishop of Bamberg. He was elected Pope Clemens II at the request of Emperor Heinrich III in 1046, but died just one year later under mysterious circumstances. The image depicts him as the ideal medieval church leader, serious and strict, in keeping with the demands of this high office.

On the second pillar, we encounter the intricate figures of Maria and Elisabeth, the "laughing angel", and, a little further, St. Dionysius, all of which were likewise created in the 13th century like the reliefs on the choir stalls. The last mentioned is the patron saint of the French, a Bishop of Paris, who was beheaded on Montmartre as a martyr in the 3rd century. According to legend, he carried his head along a considerable distance until reaching the place where St. Denis' Cathedral still stands in his honour. On the back of this third pillar, unfortunately fairly high up, is the famous Bamberg Rider (early 13th century). This is a life-size statue of a beardless man who is held to be a ruler since he is depicted on horseback with a crown. The crowning

Imperial Cathedral: The view to the west down the Early Gothic nave.
In the foreground is the cover of the Imperial Tomb.

canopy in the form of a city, the heavenly Jerusalem, shows that this former ruler was revered as a saint. This all suggests that the figure could be that of King Stephan I of Hungary (997-1038), who completed the Christianising of his country and thus was later canonised. He was also married to Gisela, a sister of Emperor Heinrich II, and thus had a connection to Bamberg. Nevertheless, however, his identity has never been established absolutely down to the present day, let alone that of the artist, who assembled 10 pieces of sandstone into a proud, nearly perfect work of art depicting the ideal of chivalry. Thus it constitutes a counterpart to the late medieval statues such as the gravestone of the aged Bishop Friedrich von Hohenlohe, which follows later in front of the West Choir.

We now enter the nave, where the Imperial Tomb stands between the stairways to the East Choir. The present-day tomb chest for Emperor Heinrich II and wife Kunigunde, both saints and founders of the Cathedral, was fashioned by the famous sculptor Tilman Riemenschneider between 1499 and 1513 from Solnhofen Marble. The cover depicts the Imperial couple life size, at their feet is depicted the separation of the couple in earthly existence due to the death of the Emperor. The side reliefs each show two scenes from

Imperial Cathedral: The Tomb Chest of Emperor Heinrich II and Empress Kunigunde, who once founded the Bishopric of Bamberg, created by T. Riemenschneider.

Cover of the tomb chest with life-size figures of the Holy Imperial Couple

legends surrounding the two saints: Whilst the Emperor's personal physician (a self-portrait by Riemenschneider?) sleeps, St. Benedict appears at night at bed of the ailing Emperor and miraculously removes a bladder stone. In the image next to this, Heinrich dreams of the weighing of his soul after his death: on one side of the Archangel Michael, the weigher of souls, devils try to tip the scales in their favor with evil deeds. A donated chalice, however, presented by St. Laurentius, tips the scales in favor of good deeds and the praying Emperor. Kunigunde's side includes a depiction of the "penny miracle" (when the craftsmen working on the Cathedral are paid, a thief is betrayed because a coin becomes red hot and bores

through his hand) as well as the divine judgement to which the Empress must submit herself (to demonstrate her marital fidelity, which has been challenged, she walks barefoot over glowing plowshares without injury). Such

The foot of the tomb: Kunigunde bids farewell to her dying husband.

36

Imperial Tomb: Kunigunde paying wages.

Imperial tomb: Archangel Michael as weigher of souls.

judgements were common in the Middle Ages and even in the subsequent centuries. In cases of doubt, the healing process after torture of this type was interpreted in order to arrive at a "just verdict".

The East Choir was dedicated to St. George and reserved for the Cathedral Chapter, for the members of which the lovely choir stalls had been made in the early 14th century. The oldest section of construction was still in late Romanesque style, which is easy to see because of the predominant round arches. From here one looks across the main sanctuary the St. Peter's Choir, the transverses and arches of which already exude the early Gothic style.

We walk through the naive toward the West Choir. Behind the fourth column, we turn to the right yet again and discover, on the outer wall, the gravestones of the Prince-Bishops Friedrich von Truhendingen (died 1366) and Albert von Wertheim (died 1421). The later is one of the most artistically valuable epitaphs of the late Middle Ages. Now we cross the nave, passing the remarkable gravestone of Prince-Bishop Friedrich von Hohenlohe (died 1352), and reach the south side of the edifice, where we turn to the right. At the end of the transept we encounter the Bamberg Altar (1523), a masterful carving by the famous artist Veit Stoß. It was the wood carver's last great work, and was originally intended to be the high altar for the Carmelite church

Imperial Cathedral: Middle relief of the "Christmas Altar", created in 1523 by the famous Nuremberg wood carver Veit Stoß

in the town of Nuremberg, where he lived and his son Andreas was Prior. He also decreed that the altar must never be coloured, may only be opened on high holy days, and shall be illuminated by not more than two candles. The motives of both the middle shrine and the two wings relate to the birth of Christ, which is why the work is also known as the "Christmas altar". In the shrine, shepherds and angels surround the holy couple; the Christ child from the original work was lost, however, and was later replaced. The reliefs at left show the Flight to Egypt and the adoration of the Magi, while the ones at right depict the birth of Maria and the presentation of Jesus in the temple. The groups of figures that once formed the upper conclusion of the shrine and wings are – although regrettably incomplete– on display in the neighbouring Diocesan Museum.

An additional monument, to Prince Bishop Philipp Graf von Henneberg (died 1487), is fastened next to the altar. The remnants of paintings can still be seen on the neighbouring choir stalls. Tucked away modestly behind is the tomb of Pope Clemens II (died 1047), the cover of which we already admitted in the Northern Aisle. This is the only extant papal grave on German soil. Of the once magnificent whole, only the sandstone base and the sides made of marble from the Austrian province of Carinthia have been preserved. The reliefs to the right and left show the four virtues bravery, wisdom, moderation, and justice; the one at head portrays St. John

Imperial Cathedral: Tomb of Pope Clemens II (died 1047), the only Papal grave north of the Alps.

the Baptist, and the one at the foot shows the Pope, to whom the Angel of Death appears in his sleep. Next to it stands the Archbishop's Chair. To the left and right in the West Choir are the intricately carved choir stalls (ca. 1400).

We walk down the North Aisle back to the Georgenchor. There are magnificent statues of the Ecclesia (the Christian church) and the synagogue on the two columns at the start of the southern choir stalls. They were once located on either side of the Prince's Portal. They date from the construction of the present-day cathedral (13th century). The church, depicted as the crowned knightly victor who once held the communion chalice and the cross in her now broken hands, does not betray her triumph with even a facial gesture. The synagogue as the personification of Jewish faith is portrayed with eyes bound, blind to the teachings of Christianity. In her right hand she holds a broken sceptre, while the tablets with the Ten Commandments are falling from her left hand.

Detail from the choir stalls: The Queen of Saba.

Choir stalls: King David playing the harp.

The three-naved crypt is preserved under the Georgenchor. Two of its capitals and the West Wall are still from the crypt of the preceding early 12th century Cathedral. Since the 19th century, it has held the sarcophagi of the first Bishops of Bamberg as well as that of King Konrad III., who died in Bamberg after returning from a Crusade in 1152 and was also laid to rest here.

A passageway leads from the South Aisle of the Cathedral to the Diocesan Museum, which is housed in the neighbouring Cathedral chapter house and the cloister of the Cathedral. It is definitely worth a visit, if only for mementoes of Emperor Heinrich II and his wife Kunigunde as well as Pope Clemens II. The numerous other precious objects in the old Cathedral Treasury were pawned or sold in bad times over the centuries and replaced by new donations. In 1553, in particular, immense demands for contributions following defeat in the "War of the Margraves" led to the loss of many valuable art objects that were melted down. The Cathedral was forced to part with much of its silver after the Seven Years' War.

Imperial Cathedral: A depiction of St. Peter, Adam and Eve before the gates of heaven, today in the Diocesan Museum.

Finally, when the Bishopric of Bamberg was dissolved in 1803, nearly all remaining and newly donated objects of value had to be handed over to the new capital city of Munich. With the exception of those items that were mementoes of Heinrich II and Kunigunde, they were auctioned off to the

Diocesan Museum:
Tues. – Sun. 10:00 AM – 5:00 PM. Closed 24-25 and 31 Dec., as well as on Fat Tuesday and Good Friday. Guided tours (except Mondays) 11:15 AM, other times by appointment.
Tel.: 0951/502325 or 502329; fax: 502320
Email: dioezesanmuseum@erzbistum-bamberg.de

benefit of the Principality of Bavaria. At least the Cathedral did recover the "Imperial Cloak" in 1851 and today it is the most valuable item in the collection of the Diocesan Museum. A tunic and a so-called "choir cloak" from the time of Heinrich II (1002-1024), as well as a cloak that belonged to a gold-embroidered rider's cloak from the 12th centuries. Other precious objects of this epoch include an ivory crucifix, a bronze candlestick, a portable altar, a gold-embroidered mitre, and the gold-plated crook of a bishop's staff. The last two objects were long attributed to St. Otto (died

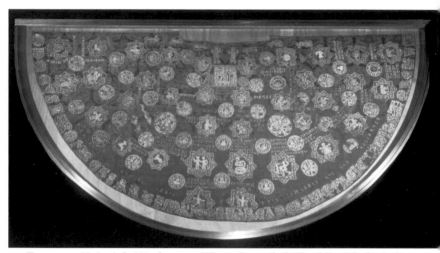

Emperor Heinrich II's famous "Star-Spangled Cloak" with depictions and inscriptions in extravagant gold embroidery.

St. Kunigunde and Heinrich's famous star-spangled cloak, all decorated with extravagant gold embroidery, are among the most valuable examples of medieval textile art. Other famous items include the large silk cloth that was discovered in the grave of Bishop Gunther (died 1065) in the floor of the Cathedral (which is known as the "Gunthertuch"), the papal hose from the tomb of Pope Clemens II (died 1047) as well as 1139), but this attribution is untenable in terms of scholarship. Some of the numerous additional items on display are on loan, have been purchased or repurchased, come from the former Court Chapel of the Prince-Bishop or the Baroque furnishings removed from the Cathedral in 1836. These are statues made of wood, metal, and stone, reliquaries in a very wide variety of forms, pictorial tapestries and paintings, altar tops

**The Bamberg
Cathedral Cross
11th-19th century**

**Silver Madonna of
the Congregation
of Mary (1696).**

**House-shaped
shrine for relics
of St. Briccius
(14th century)**

**Passion Tapestry.
Detail: Bearing of
the cross (ca. 1500)**

Votive image (1767)

and home altars, cymbals and chalices, monstrances and crucifixes, guild staffs and much more.

We exit the Cathedral through Adam's Door and walk around the church to the left. In the middle of the long side, facing the Cathedral Square, is the most intricately decorated door to the Cathedral, the Prince's Portal (1225). It was used as a splendid entrance for festive occasions. The richly populated tympanum depicts the Last Judgement, with the blessed at the left and the damned at the right. The apostles each stand on the shoulders of prophets, just as the New Testament is founded on

Imperial Cathedral: Deeply recessed walls at the Prince's Portal. Between the columns are the apostles on the shoulders of the prophets.

The Prince's Portal: Richly populated gable panel with a depiction of the Last Judgement.

the Old. They gaze astonished at the Last Judgement above them. To the side are still the columns to which the female figures of Ecclesia (left) and the synagogue mentioned earlier were attached until well into the 20th century. Attached to their columns is the figure of a Jew who a devil has blindfolded from above, making him "blind to the revelation of God".

The Old Household ⑩

Opposite the Cathedral side of the square stands the Old Household (10) of the Prince-Bishops. On the site occupied today by the three-storey Council Chambers stood, in the 10th – 11th centuries, the Imperial Palace of which the newly founded bishopric gained possession through Heinrich's donation. The building with the decorative Renaissance facade was built in 1570 under Prince-Bishop Veit von Würzburg, whose coat-of-arms (along with those of other bishops) is emblazoned on the two-storey oriel. Master Builder Erasmus Braun imortalised himself in a self-portrait at the base of the oriel. The building once served as chancellery, library, and council chambers. Since 1938, it has been home to the Museum of History, a collection covering the artistic and cultural history of the city and its environs. Besides the rooms, which are worth seeing in and of themselves, there are also numerous impressive exhibits that span the period from early history through the Middle Ages all the way up to the modern era. The oldest finds, besides numerous ceramic articles and jewellery from prehistoric times, include the "Bamberg Idols" – three statues from the 4th century, depicting an archer, a warrior, and a servant. They are probably from a prince's grave and were found in the alluvial sand of the Regnitz. Their aforementioned names were coined at a time when it was widely assumed that they were heathen sculptures that must have been dumped into the Regnitz by Christian missionaries. A late-Romanesque knight's head and a late Gothic panel painting "The Apostles' Farewell " (1483) with the oldest extant view of the City of Bamberg bear witness to Bamberg's artistic vitality and importance during the Middle Ages. A map by City Surveyor Petrus Zweidler shows the outlines of the Old Town of Bamberg in 1602 and proves that little about it has changed since then. Famous Master Builder Balthasar Neumann (1687-1753) used the wooden model exhibited when building the Pilgrimage Church "Vierzehnheiligen" above the Main River Valley at Staffelstein. Other objects of interest include the large stone Baroque and Rococo sculptures by sculptor Ferdinand Tietz, which we will encounter again later in the Rose Garden of the New Residence. Weapons, uniforms, musical instruments, and furnishings of the 19th and 20th centuries are also on exhibit.

Model for a figure of St. George to adorn the Seesbrücke, F. Tietz (ca. 1753).

Museum of History:
May – Oct.: Tues. – Sun. 9:00 AM – 5:00 PM, open Nov. – April for special exhibitions. Tel.: 0951/871142 Fax: 871464

Bamberg identifying signs that were used at the Frankfurt Trade Fair (later half of the 17th century).

The head of what was originally a full-length depiction of a knight, from before 1237

Silver tumbler found in the Regnitz near Pettstadt

Hans Baldung Grien, The Great Flood, 1516

Marksman's Prize, Nuremberg, 1712

The "Beautiful Gate" (1573), the entrance to the Old Household. Above the main portal, behind the enthroned mother of God, are Heinrich and Kunigunde, flanked by Sts. Peter and George, the patrons of the Cathedral.

To the West, the Old Residence links up with the "Beautiful Gate", created by sculptor Pankraz Wagner in 1573. Above the gateway arch, Maria is enthroned in front of a model of the Cathedral that is held by the donors, Emperor Heinrich II and Kunigunde. The central group is flanked by Sts. Peter (with keys and sword) and George (with the dragon). Both are patrons of the Cathedral. To the side are allegories for the Main and the Regnitz, which are the most important rivers for Bamberg.

Through the gate, we enter the picturesque inner courtyard of the Old Household, framed by an impressive ensemble of late Gothic residential and farm buildings dating from the 15th century. Half timbering, oriels, galleries, and various types of dormer windows break up the large wall and roof areas. Greenery and flowers make the inner courtyard look wonderfully romantic. In the summer, the buildings form an imposing backdrop for the Calderón open-air performances of the E.T.A. Hoffmann Theatre. Formerly, the buildings served a wide range of purposes in connection with running the household of Prince-Bishop: besides residential spaces and building for entertaining, the complex also encompassed the kitchen and bakery, a blaksmith's and stalls for the horses, wells, servants chambers and storage for food and fodder. Refugee families were housed here after the Second World War. The historical buildings have been and are still being restored, in part for later inclusion in the Museum of History. Other premises house the Cathedral Construction Office,

The Old Household: Self-portrait of Master Builder E. Braun at the foot of the oriel.

which deals with maintaining the centuries-old substance of the Cathedral year after year.

The Old Household, a romantic inner courtyard with farm buildings and enormous roofs. In the background are the spires of the Church of St. Michael.

Bamberg's vast Cathedral Square with the Imperial Cathedral and

the outer facades of the Old Household up to the Beautiful Gate.

The New Residence (11)

The facing sides of the Cathedral Square are formed by two of the four wings of the New Residence (11). By the late 16th century, the Old Household was no longer impressive enough for the Prince-Bishops, so in 1586 they had Geyerswörth Palace (see No. 2) refurbished as a residence. But soon this residence was also no longer in keeping with the Prince-Bishop's station. During the period 1605-11, Prince-Bishop von Gebsattel had the two western wings of the New Residence built. These were followed nearly 100 years later by the wings facing the Cathedral Square, which were built 1697-1703 under Lothar Franz von Schönborn who first, however, had to rid himself of some self-made shackles. Upon

The New Residence: In the foreground is the elevated Vierzehnheiligen Pavilion with both wings of the Schönborn Tract (1697-1703). At left in the background is one wing of the Gebsattel Tract.

his election as Prince-Bishop of Bamberg, he had namely promised the Cathedral Canons in writing that he would not start building any expensive new buildings. Once the Pope, at his urging, declared this clause invalid in 1697, the new Prince-Bishop was able to pursue his Hobby without hindrance. The building, which was designed by Court Architect Dientzenhofer, is a three-storey construction, except for a four-storey tower-like corner. It is known as the "Vierzehnheiligen Pavilion", because on a clear day you can see the pilgrimage church Vierzehnheiligen at Staffelstein from the top. Today the pavilion and the adjacent South Wing house the State Library. A staircase leads from the ground-level

The New Residence: The impressive Imperial Hall in the Schönborn Tract was used for major receptions and festivities.

New Residence:
April – Sept., open daily 9:00 AM – 6:00 PM; Oct. – Mar. Daily 9:00 AM – 4:00 PM. Closed 24 – 25 and 31 Dec., as well as on 1 Jan. and Fat Tuesday. Tel. 0951/51 93 90 Fax 51 93 91 29

centre portal to the living quarters and social areas that are open to the public, such as the Imperial Hall and the Chinese Cabinet, as well as the valuable collection of paintings. The gateway, which even then was paved with wood to minimise noise, also leads however through the Inner Courtyard to the rose garden, which is absolutely worth visiting, above all because of the grand view from here of the Michaelsberg and over the Old City all the way to the hills of the Franconian Highlands. Although it is small due to the former confines of the fortress, the garden seems spacious because of its open location. When it was created in 1705, the area was divided into then-fashionable, symmetrical fields with a very wide variety of flowers. Ferdinand Tietz's Baroque and Rococo figures were used to transform the area, giving it the appearance that it still has today. Finally, in the 19th century, it was planted in the present manner with many varieties of roses. The Pavilion (1755/65) is open as a Café in the summer. From here, one can clearly differentiate the various architectural styles between the Schönborn Tract (1697-1703, Baroque) and the nearly 100-year older Gebsattel Building (1605-11).

New Residence: The pompously furnished Chinese Cabinet was used as a small room for entertaining guests.

The Rose Garden with its many figures offers a grand view of St. Michael's Mountain.

Passing through the courtyard portal, we once again enter the broad square and imagine how the residence really should have appeared according the Prince-Bishop Lothar Franz von Schönborn's plans. He had planned a third wing, which would have run along the old outer wall to the Old Household. This would have resulted in the creation of an open courtyard of honour facing the city, as was typical in the Baroque Era. This, however, would have necessitated demolishing most of the Old Household. Fortunately, his plans never came to fruition for lack of funds.

Keeping to the right, we follow the facade of the New Residence. Where it in turns to the right, stones were removed on the Schönborn tract for the planned Southwest wing. This marks the beginning of the plain Gebsattel Tract, which adapts to the architecture of the Old Household opposite. Thus we enter the Precincts of the Cathedral Cannons, which arose in the Cathedral area starting in the 12th century and in some cases constituted the fortress-like boundary of the Domberg ("Cathedral Mountain").

This is where the Obere Karolinenstraße starts, a street which broadens to the right into a respectable green area. In the front area is a building (No. 6) with the von Wolfstein coat of arms and the year 1531; further back is the Cathedral School. To the left stands the Palace of the Archbishops' (No. 5, built 1763). In the gilt Baroque cartouche is a model of the Cathedral, borne by Emperor and Empress who sponsored it. Let us walk back a few metres along the Obere Karolinenstraße, however, and turn into the romantic Domstraße. Already at the start of the street, visitors are afforded a charming view of the alley and the cathedral spires. At their core, many of these buildings date back to the Middle Ages. A sharply arching courtyard gate, for example, bears a coat-of-arms and the year 1419; a half-timbered storey rises above it. The Baroque edifice that is house No. 5 bears the coat-of-arms of the von Greiffenclau family. The inner courtyard affords a beautiful view of the western towers. From the right, about half way up, two "cathedral cows" peek out between columns, a reference to the working animals. Further along the Domstraße at No. 7, we find half-timbered construction, oriels,

and coats-of-arms. At No. 11, "Madlers Court", there are three coats-of-arms and the year 1566.

Where the Domstraße once again leads into in the Obere Karolinenstraße, stands the former Brandenburger Hof (present version built ca. 1780). Opposite is a broad Baroque building (No. 8) that today houses the Diocesan Office of Library Operations. From 1154 on, this was the site of the Langheimer Court, the city branch of the Ebrach, Langheim und Heilsbronn monasteries, which was later used solely by the Cistercians from Langheim. Some elements dating from the Romanesque Era can still be found. The name of the restaurant, "Torschuster", and the Baroque-crowned columns on both sides of the street signal the location of the former castle gate and thus the end of the cathedral area.

Coats-of-arms of the noble building owners at the Precincts of the Cathedral Cannons.

St. Jacob's Church ⑫

On the other side of the former gate, the street broadens to form a small square that is dominated by the Baroque facade of St. Jacob's Church. The space that is open today was once taken up by the graveyard of the church, construction of which began way back in 1065 on the model of the Heinrichsdom. Careful observers will discover that there are still numerous Romantic elements behind the superimposed Baroque facade. The tower, for example, contains the oldest extant stone coat-of-arms in the town, the Meranier eagle. The Andechs-Meranier Dynasty held the Bamberg bishop's throne for many decades in the 12th and 13th centuries.

Church of St. Jacob: A figure of the Mother of God (1430) in the high altar.

Church of St. Jacob: A view through the plain Romanesque interior.

At that time the church was located outside of the Cathedral fortifications on the road used by the numerous Jacobean pilgrims on their way to Santiago de Compostela in Spain. The Romantic architectural elements inside the church are also hard to overlook: the ceiling of the three-naved basilica with its two choirs is borne up by thick pillars. The Gothic murals and the painting on the Baroque vault document the development of art styles over the

On the way to St.-Michael' s Monastery we cross the former churchyard and wander down the Michaelsbergstraße. In the valley we encounter the fifth of seven Stations of the Cross, which a wealthy citizen had erected between the Church of St. Elisabeth and St. Getreu around 1500, thus making it the oldest way of the cross in Germany. The inscription reads: "Here Christ pressed his holy face into Veronica's head cloth in front of her house. 95

The fifth station of the oldest Way of the Cross in Germany (ca. 1500).

course of the centuries. The Neo-Gothic high altar holds a Mother of God figure (1430). Some years ago now, the original statue of St. Kunigunde was moved here from the Lower Bridge for safekeeping, having been replaced by a duplicate on the bridge.

steps from Pilate's house". The sponsor was able to attest to the exact distance first hand, since he himself had paced off the distances between the individual stations in Jerusalem.

An aerial view of downtown Bamberg. In the foreground are the Monastery and Church of St. Michael, above these the Cathedral Hill

with the New Residence and the four-spired Cathedral, the course of the Regnitz River can be seen at left.

St. Michael's Monastery

From here, the street climbs rather steeply until reaching the front of the building that was once St.-Michael's Monastery (13) and is today mostly used as an old people's home known as the "Bürgerspital". An easy-to-follow plaque about the present buildings and how they are used is attached to the gateway entrance opposite the bus stop. The path leads straight from here through the spacious inner courtyard to the impressive outdoor steps in front of the Baroque facade of the church. It comes as no surprise that many young Bamberg residents choose to hold their weddings in these festive surroundings.

The baroque facade and adjoining building belie the fact that this monastery was founded way back in 1015 – just eight years after the founding of the bishopric. The first church, however, fell victim to an earthquake already in 1117. Bishop Otto the Holy (1102-1139), however, immediately had

The broad inner courtyard of the Monastery of St. Michael with one of the enormous buildings and the front of the Monastery Church above an impressive flight of steps.

The elaborate Rococo pulpit and numerous altars decorate the Church of St. Michael. Some 600 painted plants form the ceiling decoration.

a new house of worship built in the Romanesque style. Reconstruction measures in the 13th and 15th centuries, above all, however, after the catastrophic fire of 1610, did little to change the medieval monastery in its essence. In the 18th century, however, the entire monastery complex was rebuilt in Baroque style under the direction of the Dientzenhofer Brothers. The Prelate's Tract and the Gatehouses were built according to plans by Balthasar Neumann.

The outdoor steps and the decorative facade of the church including the free-standing statues are largely the contribution of the Dientzenhofer. Above the portal, angels hold a cartouche with the coat-of-arms of the monastery, the abbot (von Guttenberg), and the Prince-Bishop (von Schönborn). It is flanked by the statues of the founders of the bishopric, Heinrich II and Kunigunde. In the niches of the upper storey, the statues of Sts. Otto and Benedict frame the Mother of God. Above the clock, the figure of the patron saint of the church, the Archangel Michael, is set off against the sky.

Via the imposing outdoor steps, we reach the portal the leads us inside the church. Despite the rich Baroque appointments, the church clearly evidences the Romanesque architectural concept with the transept. The naive and aisles where erected after the fire of

1660 in the post-Gothic era. One point of interest are the nearly 600 naturalistically painted plants in the vaulting, which represent an impressive Herbarium for those times. Another noteworthy item is the pulpit (1751/52), which swings upward in very playful Rococo forms until it nearly reaches the vaulting and is considered to be one of the loveliest in Franconia. Its warm colours result from the harmonic interplay of the brown walnut and the abundant gilding. Only the disobedient angel Lucifer, plunged into the depths by the Archangel Michael, is kept in dark colours. At the edge of the canopy, the four church fathers Ambrosius, Augustine, Hieronymus und Gregory are por-

Detail of the pulpit in the Church of St. Michael

trayed, while the main body of the pulpit bears the images of the four evangelists with open books and the their respective symbols.

St. Otto's Tomb, with a hole for pilgrims to slip through

The cover of an older tomb for St. Otto.

The Baroque side altars are around twenty-five years older: at the right is the Holy Cross Altar, the Altar of St. Benedict and the Scholastics, and that of St. Kilian; at the left, the Guardian Angel altar, the Altar of Sts. Heinrich and Kunigunde, and the Altar of the popular St. Sebastian, the patron saint of protection against the much-feared plague.

Four steps lead up to the rood altar under the crossing, which is flanked by large statues of the Bamberg Emperor and Empress. Behind the rood altar, which is crowned by Eagles, is the Altar of St. Otto, which closes off the space under the high choir like a crypt. Here is the tomb of the saint, which was built in 15th century. Note the continuous opening for pious pilgrims, who even today can use this crawlspace in order to be especially close to the saint. Touching the grave is said to have a special healing effect, especially in cases of gout, rheumatism, and back trouble. The tomb is decorated by various sculptures, including another depiction of the Emperor and Empress as founders of the Cathedral. The cover, which today stands upright against the rear wall of the crypt, was once part of an earlier tomb. It shows Bishop Otto I in full vestments with book, staff, mitre, and pallium (white shoulder band with crosses). A glass reliquary holds a mitre, a chasuble and a bishop's staff. None of these, however, are from Otto's era; he was laid to rest here in the church in 1139 and was canonised 50 years later.

Via a flight of stairs we come to the Iron Grating (1730), that separates the high choir from the crossing. In the background is the enormous high altar of St. Michael. The Rococo shrine and its filigree construction form an impressive frame for J. Scheubel's painting of the enthroned Mother of God, surrounded by her flock of angels with the Archangel Michael, who conquered the demons. The Baroque choir stalls (ca. 1730) with their lovely carvings and intricate inlays are also magnificent to behold. They were made even more elaborate in the mid 18th century by rich Rococo carving, which in turn offers a spirited framework for three paintings each. The painting depict the four great early fathers of the church, King David, and a scene from the mountain of olives.

A door at the end of the right aisle leads to the Chapel of the Holy Sepulchre, the medieval core of which is scarcely discernible due to heavy modification during the Baroque Period. Christ's Sepulchre (18th century) is covered by roof-like vaulting and crowned by a globe with a snake, God the Father and the Dove of the Holy Spirit. Inside the corpse is attended by four watchers, outside by four angels. The stucco ceiling of the chapel is also remarkable; it is decorated with nume-

Church of St. Michael: Chapel of the Holy Tomb in Baroque style.

A detail from the "Dance of Death" in the Chapel of the Holy Tomb

From the nave we now regard the richly ornamented organ front, which was created in the style of the later Renaissance shortly after the fire of 1610. Statues of Sts. Otto and Benedict. are on watch next to the organ pipes. In the entranceway are 28 wooded panels with scenes from the life of St. Otto. They were created in 1628 – at the time of the Counter-Reformation – to decorate the saint's grave. One of the panels shows Otto's grave as it was at the time.

rous scenes from a dance of death: death takes the rich and the poor, the young and the old, the sick and the able-bodied. However, death also reflects on itself (while contemplating a skull) and blows soap bubbles to pass the time.

Right after leaving the chapel, we first glance back at the right transept: Under a wooden gallery stands an ancillary altar with depictions of Benedictine saints. In the left transept, the corresponding altar with numerous figures shows the church triumphant in conflict. Here is the entrance to the Sacristy, flanked by a man of sorrows ("Christ the Merciful", ca. 1350) and a Baroque grieving Madonna. Numerous elaborate gravestones of Bamberg Prince-Bishops during the period 1556-1779 are distributed along the two aisles. They once stood in the cathedral until they were removed in 1830.

A view of the monastery courtyard from the steps outside the Church of St. Michael

From the steps outside the church we a glance across the large inner courtyard. Today the city uses the long building to the left and the one opposite as an old people's home. These buildings, which once belonged to the farm, were planned and built in the 18th century with the participation of the famous architect Balthasar Neumann. To the right, the end of the Prelate's Building adjoins the wing of the former Monastery Brewery, which today houses the Franconian Brewery Museum. It exhibits an extensive collection of equipment and documents from the history of beer brewing and modern processes from making malt to beer that is ready for sale. The historic ice cellar of the brewery, which had to preserve the costly ice during the warm season, is also open to the public. The brewery was mentioned in official records as early as 1122 and is thus the oldest of the once numerous breweries in Bamberg. Today there is a beer garden at the end of this building.

We keep to the right and – passing by the beer garden – enter what was formerly the monastery garden. Passing another wing of the old people's home, we walk by a garden gate and the Café Michelsberg before, at the end of the terrace, enjoying a lovely view of, above all, the Cathedral district. Visitors who want to enjoy this view even more intensely should take a quick side trip to the right to visit the terrace café, the

Brewery Museum: Traditional equipment and furnishings of the brewers' trade

Franconian Brewery Museum:
April – Oct.: Wed. – Sunday 1:00 – 5:00 PM. Closed Good Friday.
Tel.: 0951/53016 Fax: 52540

observation point, and the view of the Cathedral from the outermost corner of the spacious park.

Others will begin to descend St. Michael's Mountain at the outer left corner of the terrace, which is marked by a white metal cross. At the end of the steps we keep to the right and follow the footpath toward "Stadtmitte" ("City Centre"). At the foot of the high retaining wall of the rose garden, the footpath leads into a small street that leads downhill toward the Regnitz River. We pass a coat-of-arms on the wall and, at the end of the wall, a gateway with a cartouche and a coat-of-arms at the entrance to Residenzstraße. After walking down the Elisabethenstraße a few steps we come to a small square with the dainty Church of St. Elisabeth. Other objects of interest at the edges of the square include the Fountain of St. Francis and a sandstone relief, the first station of Germany's oldest Way of the Cross (ca. 1500) mentioned elsewhere in this book. The inscription reads: "Here Christ was taken away from Pilate's house bearing his cross". The church itself was consecrated in 1554 and belonged to Heiliggeistspital (1328), later Elisabethenspital. After dissolution of church property, the church served as a warehouse until the City of Bamberg purchased it in 1877 and refurbished it in keeping with its original purpose. Today the neighbouring building in the complex is used as a prison.

Little Venice (14)

Back on the Elisabethenstraße, there is a pleasant half-timbered house on the corner where this street crosses Oberen Sandstraße. After just a few steps along Elisabethenstraße, we reach the banks of the Regnitz. From here we enjoy a unique view of the rows of houses on the opposite bank, known as Little Venice (14). The picturesque ensemble of little fishermen's houses makes a pleasant impression with high roofs and numerous gables, decorative facades with balconies, arbours, and tiny front gardens in which there are landing places for the fishing boats.

Between the barred windows of the prison and the river, we continue on our way toward the city centre until the street "Am Leinritt" ends. Opposite us is the last building of the fishermen's quarter, the broad Old Slaughterhouse. To the right of this, in front of the larger of the two iron cranes, is the landing place for passenger boats for tours on the Regnitz and the Main-Danube canal.

View across the Regnitz from the Markusbrücke, at left the romantic rows of one-time fishermen's houses, known as "Little Venice".

The Kasernstraße now takes us away from the riverbank. At the intersection with Dominikanerstraße stands the stately Schrottenberg Palace off to the right; to the left, in the background, one can make out the Dominican Church. Above the intersection, we come to Obere Sandstraße. Off to the right, small shops and cosy restaurants invite us to interrupt our tour for a moment, which we then continue toward the left. The Baroque house at No. 8 has a pleasant panel with coats-of-arms, held by two gilt lions, and a lovely sculpture of the Madonna. The neighbouring, interesting half-timbered facade with the elaborate cantilevers belongs to the taproom of the "Heller" Brewery. The down-to-earth pub is called "Zum Schlenkerla" after an earlier publican who, as it so happens, supposedly always dangled his arms when walking. Today the word is also used for the mug in

Resting on the banks of the Regnitz with a view of Little Venice.

which the dark Rauchbier ("smoky beer"), a Bamberg speciality, is served. The Baroque building in the extension of the half-timbered structure is also belongs to the brewery taproom. The historic pub and brewery "Zum Ringlein", opposite, was mentioned already in 1545 and today still unites beer

making and selling, as many bars and restaurants in Bamberg once did.

The "Domstuben" building, which belongs to the "Heller" brewery, is adjoined by the plain Dominican Church. On its front side there is only a small relief with a crucifix and a depiction of St. Christopher

Historic half-timbered facades in Bamberg's Old Town

A statue of St. Kunigunde on the Lower Bridge.

above the portal. Before turning into the street Dominikanerstraße along the front side of the church, let us pause to cast a glance back along the broad Herrenstraße. The large Baroque building in the background is especially striking, with just four large, coloured statues facing the plaza-like street. The Dominikanerstraße, however, brings us in a few paces to the Lower Bridge, which spans the left fork of the Regnitz here, which used to be part of the old Ludwig-Danube-Main canal. From here, Bamberg's favourite saint,

Kunigunde, looks down from her high pedestal with a gentle smile upon the ornately painted Bridge Town Hall. Plaques here commemorate the victims of the Third Reich: fallen soldiers and deported and murdered Jews alike.

The longest leg of our tour, which has taken us above all through the Bishop's Town and around the Old Town Hall, ends here at the Isle Town Hall. There is a much shorter route, passing above all through Bamberg's shopping streets, which we can use to round out our tour.

A Short Tour of the Isle City

After leaving the Lower Bridge, we follow the banks of the Regnitz toward the Old Slaughterhouse. The two iron cranes indicate that this was once the landing for freighters on the Old Canal. Today the only boats that stop here are, as mentioned above, passenger boats on tours.

The front and gables of the Old Slaughterhouse (1741/42) face the square with the cranes. One long side is built with arcades over the river, which made it easy to dump blood and waste from butchering into the water, as was common in that day. The complicated Latin inscription above the oxen draws a

One of the two old iron cranes at the landing place. To the right is a corner of the Old Slaughterhouse.

Boat tours:
Regnitz and Main-Danube Canal:
March – Oct., daily every hour on the hour, starting at 11:00 AM.
Tel. 0951/26679
Boat trips on the Main:
July – Sept. Sun., Wed., Fri. Departing Bamberg for Volkach at 8:30
AM. Tel.: 09321/91810

connection between the profane functional building and its modern use as a repository for books and documents belonging to the University of Bamberg. Fortunately, the translation is inscribed under the adjacent windows: "To be an ox without having been a calf before is an affront to nature, but it is happening in my case, since the artist's hand has made me an ox, before nature had even made a calf of me".

Dürer, who took up quarters here in what was then the inn "Wilder Mann". House No. 29 is home to the "Museum of Early Islamic Art" one of the smaller of Bamberg's fourteen museums.

We leave the banks of the Regnitz following the route Austraße/An der Universität. The street is flanked by historic buildings on both sides, some of which were once

A Medieval-looking inner courtyard in Kapuzinerstraße.

The so-called "Wedding House" opposite was built by the city in Renaissance style 1610-12. Wealthy citizens could rent this house to hold festivities. Unfortunately, the city only had the building patched up following damage incurred during the Second World War. Today the University of Bamberg uses it as an academic building. We around back of the building in the street known as Austraße, where there is a plaque commemorating a visit by the famous artist Albrecht

used as a college by the Jesuits and today house parts of the University of Bamberg. A sign calls attention to one of Germany's oldest museums, the Bamberg Museum of Natural History. Established in 1795, it exhibits a remarkable collection of rare animal specimens, fossils, and minerals amidst classical furnishings. The street ends in the picturesque Haymarket, which is surrounded by historic facades from a wide variety of epochs.

Am Maxplatz ⑮

The extension of the Frauengasse leads us to the next intersection, where, turning right we reach the broad square known as Maxplatz (15). It is bounded to the north by the one-time Theological Seminary, today the Town Hall. To the south, it is bounded by the former St. Katharine's Hospital, which today contains residences, a department store, and other businesses. Prince-Bishop Friedrich Karl von Schönborn (1729-46) had his Court Master Builder Balthasar Neumann plan and build both massive buildings. During the late 19th century, a fountain was erected on the square with five sculptures from the history of Bamberg: King Max I Joseph of Bavaria, surrounded by Emperor Heinrich II, his wife Kunigunde, Bishop Otto I, and King Conrad III, who was laid to rest in Bamberg Cathedral.

The uniform Baroque architecture continues behind Maxplatz in the Hauptwachstraße, which we follow briefly to the left. The street is named after the harmonious Baroque building opposite Maxplatz, the Hauptwache (1774). As late as the 18th century, next to this

Maxplatz:
A market in front of
the statute of King
Maximilian I Joseph
of Bavaria.

Museum of Natural History: *April – Sept- Tues.-Sun. 9 AM – 5 PM;*
Oct. – March Tues.-Sun. 10 AM – 4 PM. Tel.: 0951/8631248 Fax: 8631250
Gardeners' and Hoer's Museum: *May – Oct. Wed. and Sun. 2:00 –*
5:00 PM, Tel. 0951/31477
Museum of Early History: *May – Oct. Tues. – Sun. 9:00 AM – 5:00 PM,*
Tel. 0951/871142 Fax: 871464

building decorated with figures there was a city gate in the direction of the nearby right fork of the Regnitz. Starting in 1960, this fork of the river was expanded to form the Rhein-Main-Danube Canal. On the other side of the canal, in the direction of the railway station, is what at its heart is Bamberg's oldest church, the Church of St. Gangolf. Another sight worth mentioning is the Gardener's and Hoer's Museum (a typical gardener's house with equipment and furnishings reflecting the life and work of this occupational group) in the Mittelstraße.

St. Martin's Church ⑯

We remain in the pedestrian precincts and turn again toward town centre. The Maxplatz, mentioned already above, does not show any signs that the Church of St. Martin and its churchyard were located here until 1805. Today, flower and vegetable markets are held daily here and on the adjoining part of the Green Market. The name St. Martin's Church (16) was taken over by the nearby, former Jesuit church, which immediately appears off to our right ahead. This church has a facade that is typical for churches of this order in the Baroque Era. It was designed by Georg Dientzenhofer in the late 17th century and modelled on the Jesuit St. Martin's Church in Munich. Sights especially worth seeing include the painted fake copula (Francesco Marchini, 1716), which one should view both directly from below and from the altar. The painting pleased the

A view across the Green Market to the decorative facade of the Church of St. Martin.

Church of St. Martin. Numerous side altars lead one's gaze toward the choir and the high altar of the former Jesuit church.

Prince-Bishops and the rich citizens of the town very much and the artist was swamped with subsequent orders. A medieval piece from the old St. Martin's Church found its way into the new church: a vesper scene (ca. 1330), that is installed in the side altar. It shows the smiling mother of God with her dead son, Christ the Redeemer. The old devotional picture of the church, "Maria's Comfort" (15th century), can be seen directly below the aforementioned one.

We continue our journey along the pedestrian precinct. The broad Baroque buildings attest to the financial power of the citizenry here in the 18th century. The

"Stapf'sche Haus" (No. 7), in particular, puts one in mind of the New Residence of the Archbishops.

Vesper image (ca. 1330): The Mother of God and the Redeemer

Where the street broadens into a genuine market square, there is a pleasant fountain (1698) with a figure of Neptune, God of the Sea. Locals refer to it irreverently and lovingly as the "Gabelmanns-brunnen" or "Forkman's Fountain". Here we are in the town centre of Bamberg, where young people and adults, shoppers and strollers meet. From here it is just at few metres to the Bridge Town Hall and Geyerswörth Palace, the start and finish of both of our walking tours.

The "Forkman's Fountain" at the Green Market.

A view from the Isle Town of the Upper Bridge and the Old Town Hall with the Baroque encased spire.

Altenburg Fortress ⑰

Altenburg Fortress, which is visible from many places in the city, is situated on the highest of Bamberg's seven hills (386 m above sea level). The last leg of the approx. 3 km long footpath is fairly steep and difficult going, so

The fortress was already mentioned as property of the Religious Foundation of St. Jacob in an official document dating from 1109. In 1124, Bishop Otto the Holy consecrated the fortress chapel. Starting in the mid 13th century,

An aerial view of Fortress Altenburg, once the refuge of the Prince-Bishops of Bamberg.

it is definitely worth taking a regularly scheduled bus (Rennersteig stop) or driving there by car. There is generally ample parking for motorists next to the fortress; if need be, one can also park a little before reaching the top.

the Prince-Bishops used it as a refuge and fortress of last resort. Later it was also used as a residence a richly furnished with art treasures. Albrecht Dürer and Dr. Faust stayed here in 1505, during the regency of Bishop Georg III

Altenburgverein:
Tel. 09 51/5 33 87, Fax 09 51/5 09 06 63
Homepage: www.altenburgverein.de

Schenk von Limpurg. During the 1553 War of the Margraves, the infamous Albrecht Alcibiades von Brandenburg-Kulmbach, known as "the Wild Margrave", had it plundered and largely destroyed. All that remains of the medieval buildings is the 33-m high keep (13th century) and parts of the ring wall. At the top of the tower, there still hangs an iron basket that was once used to send fire signals to Fortress Giechburg (near Scheßlitz) 20 km away. The name of the lounge "Hoffmannsklause" in the new building of the former palace commemorates E.T.A. Hoffmann's 1812 stay at the fortress. The observation terrace offers visitors a magnificent view of the bishop's see and it environs.

Altenburg. A romantic view of historic buildings and Romantic revivals.

Altenburg: The imposing entrance to the fortress with enormous keep.

Day Trips in the Region

Seehof Palace

Just three kilometres northeast of Bamberg, near Memmelsdorf, is Seehof Palace. The Prince-Bishops of Bamberg bought the once watery terrain from the Baron von Rotenhan zu Rentweinsdorf in 1489 and first had a "Princely House" built there, 1687 as a hunting and summer residence. The enclosed four-wing structure with corner towers crowned by cupolas leaves one with the impression of a fortress, and thus is also know as "Marquardsburg" ("Marquard's Fortress"), although only rough construction was com-

An aerial view of Seehof Palace: Located in a watery region, the Prince-Bishops used it as a hunting palace and summer residence.

which, however, was ruined during the Thirty Years' War. Prince-Bishop Marquard Sebastian Schenk von Stauffenberg had the present-day palace built starting in pleted during the lifetime of the building owner. Some of the social areas created after 1700, according to plans by Balthasar Neumann, among others, are

Seehof Palace: *Guided tours 15 April – 31 October (except Mondays) 2:00 – 4:00 PM. Group tours: other times by appointment. Tel. 0951/4095-42 Fax: -30*
Cascade: *1 May – 3 Oct. hourly 11:00 AM – 4:00 PM for 10 minutes*

worth seeing. Above all, the Rococo Banqueting Hall with its artistic stuccowork and the magnificent ceiling fresco "Heaven of the Gods" (1752, Giuseppe Appiani). At one time, the Palace Park was also a famous attraction, with grottoes, fountains of all kinds, and hundreds of Rococo sculptures. Today the Park has been re-landscaped, for the most part, and decorated with a few remaining sculptures. The now refurbished buildings house a branch office of the State Bureau for the Preservation of Historic Buildings and Monuments.

A Rococo sculpture in the park at Seehof Palace.

Baroque fountains before the impressive backdrop of Seehof Palace

The famous pilgrimage church "Vierzehnheiligen" ("Fourteen Saints") located in heavily wooded surroundings near Staffelstein.

Staffelstein, Vierzehnheiligen, and Banz Monastery

Federal Route B 173 leads northward from Bamberg to Staffelstein (25 km), birthplace of the most famous German master of arithmetic, Adam Riese (1492-1559). No buildings survive from the period during which he lived, however, since a disastrous city fire destroyed the entire town centre in 1684. For that, however, numerous pretty half-timbered houses survive from the period of reconstruction. These are primarily grouped around the interesting Town Hall.

Just 2 kilometres northeast of Staffelstein is a special jewel of Baroque ecclesiastical architecture, Vierzehnheiligen Pilgrimage Church, a point of attraction for both the faithful and lovers of sacred art. The founding of the church can be traced back to visions experienced by a shepherd from Langheim at this spot in the years 1445/46. An altar was erected here, surrounded by a church that was consecrated already in 1448. It became a much visited place of pil-

A view of Pilgrimage Church Vierzehnheiligen with the central altar of grace.

grimage, for it was the first place of devotion in which one could beseech all of the fourteen saints known as the "holy helpers" at the same time.

After the first church became dilapidated, in 1741 the cornerstone was laid for a new church according to plans by Architect Balthasar Neumann. Contrary to this plan, Construction Supervisor Krohne moved the church so that the glass-enclosed, sacred patch of ground was located in the nave. It was only this move that permitted the generous division of space around the centrally located, free-standing altar of grace which today calls forth astonished respect in visitors. The richly populated superstructure with statues of the fourteen "holy helpers" and the crowning Christ child was created in Rococo style in 1768 by the Wessobrunn stucco artists Johann Michael and Franz Xaver Feichtmayr as well as

Johann Georg Übelher.

Although there is a direct line of sight between them, there are still 5 kilometres of road separating the pilgrimage church and Banz Monastery. This was once the site of the castle of the Margrave of Schweinfurt. The castle was converted into a monastery starting in 1071. The present day complex was built 1698-1708 under Master Builder Leonhard Dientzenhofer; the church (1710-19), construction of which was supervised by his younger brother Johann, is built in the style of the Italian Baroque. The church interior dispenses with straight lines almost altogether and yet offers an impression of absolute harmony upon entering the church. Unlike at "Vierzehnheiligen", the large ceiling frescos have been preserved in the original colours. The side altars at the transition to the choir are dedicated to the Three Wise Men and the fourteen "holy helpers" respectively, another proof of the harmony between the monastery and the pilgrimage church opposite it. Tucked away behind the enormous high altar – with monastic father Benedict in the halo– are the elaborate choir stalls (1749/50): 34 inlaid pictures fashioned from various types of wood, ivory, mother-of-pearl, and silver tell the story of St. Benedict's life and works.

The Benedictine Monastery of Banz overlooking the Main river valley

Weißenstein Palace

Twenty-three kilometres south of Bamberg, Prince-Bishop Lothar Franz von Schönborn had a summer residence built for his family during the period 1711-18. The last Truchsess of Pommersfelden (the "Truchsess" was a royal official responsible for kitchen and board) died without an heir in 1710, and his estate devolved to the Schönborn dynasty, in whose possession it remains today. Under the direction of Royal Master Builder Johann Dientzenhofer, who was much assisted in the planning phase by Johann Lukas von Hildebrandt of Vienna, Master Builder Maximilian Welsch of Mainz, and the building owner himself, a spacious three-wing complex was erected in the then popular style. Pavilion-type elements emphasise the transitions between and ends of the wings, even more so dramatically in the middle of the main wing. The curve of the low stables opposite, planned by Maximilian von Welsch, makes a charming contrast to the residential building.

The dominant middle tract holds the

Weißenstein Palace: Behind the facade in the middle part of the main wing is the magnificent staircase.

Weißenstein Palace: *April – Oct., guided tours Tues. – Sun. at 9:00, 10:00, and 11:00 AM and 2:00, 3:00, and 4:00 PM. Short tours at 11:30 AM and 4:30 PM. Tel. 09548/98180*

The famous double staircase in the private palace of Prince-Bishop Lothar Franz von Schönborn.

magnificent three-story staircase, one of the most famous of the Baroque Era. Behind this, at ground-floor level, is the grotto-like Garden Hall. Above it, the large Banquet Hall, also known as the Marble Hall because of its handsome marble appointments, extends across the upper two storeys. Magnificent columns and pillars of stucco marble divide the walls and guide the eye to the 15-m high ceiling, on which the triumph of the virtues over the vices is depicted in a glorifying manner. To the east, facing the Palace Park, this tract adjoins the royal apartments. The Hall of Mirrors is especially magnificent; it is located behind the bedroom in the Northeast corner of the tract. Parallel to the royal apartments, facing the courtyard of honour, are the Grand Gallery and additional gallery spaces in which the Schönborn Dynasty's collection of splendidly executed paintings is exhibited. The collection includes works of Dutch, Italian, and German painters of the 16th – 18th centuries.

Ebrach Monastery, located approx. 35 km west of Bamberg via the B 22, is also a rewarding place to visit. The most impressive things about this complex, the oldest Cistercian monastery east of the Rhine, are the self-contained nature of the Baroque monastery complex and the monuments of Würzburg bishops (13th century), Queen Gertrud of the Staufer Dynasty (the wife of King Conrad III.), and her son Friedrich von Rothenburg.

Scheduled Events

Bamberg offers it citizens and guests a richly varied cultural program year round. It starts at Easter with the presentation of passion crèches in the Maternkapelle and continues with concerts at Seehof Palace (with the Bamberg String Quartet), the Ancient Music and New Music Days, and the Residence Festival (soloists of the Bamberg Symphony in concert in the Imperial Hall of the New Residence) in May and June. Free public organ recitals are given Saturdays from May until October, from Noon until 12.30 PM in the Imperial Cathedral.

June is marked by the highly traditional Corpus Christi procession

Madonna on the high altar of the "Upper Parish Church".

Corpus Christi procession with a Madonna statue on the way from the Upper Parish Church to the Isle Town.

and the Franconian Wine Festival, as well as the start of the well-known Calderón outdoor performances of the E.T.A. Hoffmann Theatre in the inner courtyard of the Old Residence, which continue on into July. Then they receive competition from the Brewery Nostalgia Festival (pedestrian precinct), the summer concert season of the famous Bamberg Symphony, and the summer serenades at Seehof Palace (featuring, among others, the Bamberg String Quartet). August is marked by the Bamberg Antique Weeks and, on the first weekend of the month, the biggest public festival in Bamberg, known as the Sandkerwa (Old Town area).

The Bamberg Cabaret Days (October until December) then

lead to the final highlight of the year, when the Christmas Market (Maximiliansplatz) and the Bamberg Way of the Crèche draw thousands of visitors to this city of international cultural importance between the first Sunday in Advent and the 6th of January.

Besides these fixed events, Bamberg also hosts concerts by the Capella Antiqua Bambergensis, the Bamberg Baroque Ensemble, and the Musica Canterey, Rose Garden Serenades and a Satire Festival, performances at Lohse's Marionette Theatre and the Brentano Theatre, and a medieval market in the inner courtyard of Geyerswörth Palace.

One highpoint of the annual "Sandkerwa" public festival is the "boat jousting" competition before the picturesque backdrop of Little Venice.

Bamberg – City of Crèches

Since the late eighties, Bamberg has borne besides the honorary names "the Rome of Franconia" and "International Cultural Treasure" an additional illustrious epithet, the "City of Crèches". The Jesuits introduced the idea of crèche building to the city already nearly four centuries ago. The "Association of Bamberg Crèche Enthusiasts", which breathed new life into this traditional idea, was founded in 1919. In particular, the Crèche-Building School founded by this association more than twenty years ago has helped to disseminate this form of Christian tradition in Bamberg and its environs.

A Bamberg crèche in the Upper Parish Church: Scene with shepherds.

A Bamberg crèche in the Upper Parish Church: the Adoration of the Magi

More than 30 of these groups of figures are among the exhibits of the "Bamberg Way of the Crèche", which are set up in public squares, churches, museums, and banks. Persons exploring the city between the first Sunday in Advent and Epiphany (6 January) will be rewarded by the sight of many and various masterful representations of the wonder of Holy Night. Artistically talented, skilled master crèche builders have turned their nearly boundless fantasy to the task of creating ever new interpretations of the miraculous events of that night: in wood, ceramics, or porcelain, modern or Baroque, Franconian or Oriental in design, sometime life-sized, sometimes as miniatures.

The two crèches with life-sized figures at Schönleinsplatz and Maxplatz already garnered prizes in European competitions for large crèches in the past years by virtue of their masterfully artistic craftsmanship. Related sights of note include the collections in the Diocesan Museum (from the Baroque Era to the present day) and in the Maternkapelle (works by the local crèche building school) as well as the richly populated depictions in the Carmelite Church and the Church of St. Martin (200 wooden figures). Besides the modern crèche in the Cathedral, visitors should also, by way of comparison, view the Christmas Altar in the South Transept, which was created in 1523 by the world-famous Nuremberg wood-carver Veit Stoß.

Christmas crèche in the Cathedral: The Angel of the Annunciation with Maria

Crèche in the Cathedral: the Adoration of the Magi in the stall at Bethlehem

Hours of opening and tours:
Tourist and Congress Service
Geyerswörthstraße 3 · Tel. 0951/2976-310 and 2976-200 (-204)

Practical Information from A to Z

Information

Important Telephone Numbers:

ADAC motorists' breakdown service:	01802/222222
Bamberg Transit Authority:	77715
Medical emergency no.:	56565
German Rail timetable info:	19419
Fire brigade emergency no.:	112
Lost property office:	871268
Police emergency no.:	110
Bamberg police headquarters:	871268
Medical service/chemist's:	19222
City administration:	870

Bamberg telephone area code: 0951

Airfield:
Aero Club, Zeppelinstr. 17, Tel. 871161

Arrival and Hotel Reservations:
Tourism & Congress Service,
Tourist Information
Geyerswörthstr. 3, 96047 Bamberg,
Tel. 2976-200 bis -204, Fax 2976-222
Email: touristinfo@bamberg.info
Internet: www.bamberg.info
Office hours (Tourist Information):
Mon. - Fri. 9:30 AM – 6:00 PM, Sat. 9:30
AM – 2:30 PM; April - Dec.,
additionally Sun. 9:30 AM – 2:30 PM.
Fat Tuesday, 24 and 31 Dec 9:30 AM –
12:30 PM. Closed on Good Friday,
1 Nov, 25 and 26 Dec.
Accommodation Office: Tel. Tel. 2976-310

Bicycles for Hire:
Tel. 23012, Tel. 12428, Tel. 22967,
Tel. 130388, Tel. 203477

Boats for Hire:
Info U. Wagner, Tel. 26165

Bus Parking:
P 1: Pfeuferstraße · P 2: Mußstraße
P 3: Margaretendamm · P 4:
Lichthaidenstr.
P 5: Heinrichsdamm (Alter Plärrer)

Campgrounds:
Island, Am Campingplatz 1,
96049 Bamberg-Bug, Tel. 56320

Caravan Parking:
Heinrichsdamm Park & Ride (P 5)

Cinemas:
Kino & Cafe Lichtspiel, Untere
Königstraße 34, Tel. 26785. City-
Kinozentrum, Luitpoldstraße 52,
Tel. 27024

Cathedral-Tourism:
Domplatz 5, Tel. 502 330, Fax 502 320

International Artists' House:
Unterer Kaulberg 4, 96049 Bamberg,
Tel. 95501-0; Fax 95501-29

Lost Property Office:
Mon.-Fri. 9:00 – Noon, Rathaus (Town
Hall), Am Maxplatz 3,
Room 125/First Floor, Tel. 871268

Port of Bamberg:
Port Authority: Tel. 965050

Post Offices:
Ludwigstr. 25 (near the train station),
Gaustadter Hauptstr. 46, Heinrichstr. 1,
Seehofstr. 26, St.-Wolfgang-Platz 1

Public Transit:
Bamberg Transit Authority: Tel. 77257
Omnibusverkehr Franken: Tel. 76009

Swimming:
Städtisches Hallenbad (Municipal Indoor
Swimming Pool), Margaretendamm 5.
Outdoor pools:
Stadionbad, Pödeldorfer Str. 176,
Gaustadt, Badstr. 17,
Hainbad, Zinkenwörth 18

Ticket Reservations:
E.T.A.-Hoffmann Theatre Box Office
Tel. 87143331. BVD Ticket Service and
Travel Agency, Lange Straße 22,
Tel. 9808220.
Ticket Kiosk, Untere Königstraße 40,
Tel. 23837

Youth Hostel:
Wolfsschlucht, Oberer Leinritt 70,
Tel. 56002; Fax 55211